Other works by Glenn Colquhoun

Poetry:
The art of walking upright
An explanation of poetry to my father
How we fell

Children's books:
Uncle Glenn and me
Uncle Glenn and me too
Mr Short, Mr Thin, Mr Bald and Mr Dog

Essay:
Jumping ship

PLAYING GOD

for Mrs Hall

PLAYING GOD
poems about medicine

Glenn Colquhoun

Hammersmith Press
London, UK

First published in 2002 by Steele Roberts, Wellington, Aotearoa
New Zealand.

Revised edition first published in Great Britain 2007 by
Hammersmith Press Limited, 496 Fulham Palace Road, London
SW6 6JD, UK

www.hammersmithpress.co.uk

with the assistance of Seth Rankin

British Library Cataloguing in Publication Data:
A CIP record of this book is available from the British Library.

ISBN 978-1-905140-16-9

Designed by Amina Dudhia
Typeset by Julie Bennett, Bespoke Publishing Ltd
Production by Helen Whitehorn, Pathmedia
Printed and bound by TJ International Ltd, of Padstow,
Cornwall, UK

First page illustration: 15th century deathbed scene.
From Costume Historique, Racinet, Mary Evans Picture Library

Cover kowhaiwhai (pattern strip) artist: Ross Hemara

Contents

List of illustrations

Introduction

I am an ambivalent doctor. I think sometimes that the god of medicine is a cantankerous old bitch in the sky. At times she tries to woo me. She allows me the most intense and beautiful views of human life. At other times she terrifies me by revealing my limitations as well as her ability to deal so arbitrarily with our existence.

But I am a shallow man. The pay is good. The special treatment is difficult to ignore. The knowledge is fascinating. The toys are exhilarating. The stories are addictive. The opportunity to stand inside the red-hot zone of another human being is pretty much beyond compare.

I am charmed by the ledge I am offered every day on which to stand and look at what it is to be alive.

I am hurt because I am scared that one day I will be found out for the fraud that I am. I am not a god able to fix everything I want to. I am a human being with a little bit of science and a lot of doubt who relies greatly on three things: the body's ability to heal itself, my patients' belief in my profession and being polite to as many people as I can.

The truth is that I both love and hate medicine. I don't know how long I will live with her or she with me. I have always stayed for the beauty I have seen in my patients and for the time it has taken me to write these poems. They have been a long conversation with my doubt, trying to work out my angst and finally come to some peace with this beautiful, old hag I have married.

To everyone who has ever been a patient of mine thank-you for the absolute privilege. Thank-you for your trust and kindness. Thank-you for your vulnerability and laughter and entertainment. Thank-you for the poetry. You have no idea how many times you have healed me.

PATIENTS I HAVE KNOWN

At Thasos, Philistes had a headache for a long time and on falling into a state of stupor one day took to his bed ...

The unmarried daughter of Euryanax took a fever ...

Pythion who lived near the temple of Earth suffered from twitching which began in the hands ...

At Larissa a bald man suddenly had a pain in the right thigh...

   ~ *Epidemics Book III*, Hippocrates.

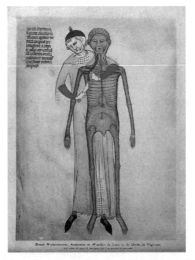

Illustrations of dissection, from *Liber Notabilium Philippi VI*, 'Anathomia' by Guido de Papia, 1345. Wellcome Library, London.

A history

The presenting complaint

It was a fine day. I was outside. I thought to myself it was a good day for washing. There are people who say they will do it for me but there are many ways of hanging it out. It was a fine day and I was warm. It was a terrible sound. Like someone had cracked a branch. I knew by the sound of it that it wasn't good. It was a very hot day. I hope someone has got them in. You probably don't mind which way they are hung.

A past medical history

I knew a doctor once which was many years ago. You may have heard of him. You have not. You must have. He was quite famous. He invented a machine. I was the first he tried it on. Do they still use it? I'm not surprised.

No. I have no problems there. I take pills of course but I don't know what they are for. They may be for that. I have read that sometimes you would not know. They could be for that — the pills. It would make sense. What do you think?

No. No. No. No. Oh my goodness no. I have never had that. Not at least that I know of. Should I have known? I am not sure. I could have I suppose. How would I know? I wouldn't have thought so. You have me thinking.

You have had me thinking and now I remember. I have had upsets there yes. In the past. Yes I have had problems. How is that then? I have. Thank you for reminding me.

The medications

I have taken many pills in my time. Yes there have been a lot. I used to take a blue pill. It was small even for a pill. Once for a while I took the blue-tongued mussel. Have you ever heard of that? I don't know why I took it now. I told my doctor I had been taking it. He said the less of it I took the better. I don't suppose I should have taken it now. The blue-tongued mussel. Could it have done me any harm?

The allergies

I am allergic to morphine. I must not have it. They gave it to me when I came here. It made me see things. There was a room full of men and they were looking at me. One of them I thought quite smart. He asked me to dance. I said to the doctor could I dance? My leg was not sore. I said the men had been talking to me and did he think what they had been saying could be true? He asked me which men? I said the men who asked me to dance. He said I was not to have any more. I was disappointed. He did not see them at all.

A social history

I have been married. It did not seem long ago. I met him when he was playing rugby and I was going to church. In the end of course he came to church. I had to wait until he could not play any more. He went happily after that. He came to be very strong. He was an elder. He was a winger and an elder. Very fast. I suppose I was faster.

I live on my own now and I do not smoke. My husband used a pipe. Is that better or worse? He said it was better. I was not sure. I drink wine on occasions. I have been told that it is good for me.

You have been very thorough.

Have I told you what you wanted to know?

She asked me if she took one pill for her heart and one pill for her hips and one pill for her chest and one pill for her blood how come they would all know which part of her body they should go to

I explained to her that active metabolites in each pharmaceutical would adopt a spatial configuration leading to an exact interface with receptor molecules on the cellular surfaces of the target structures involved.

She told me not to bullshit her.

I told her that each pill had a different shape and that each part of her body had a different shape and that her pills could only work when both these shapes could fit together.

She said I had no right to talk about the shape of her body.

I said that each pill was a key and that her body was ten thousand locks.

She said she wasn't going to swallow that.

I told her that they worked by magic.

She asked me why I didn't say that in the first place.

When

He smiled

He saw seagulls wait

On the telephone wires

At the corners of his eyes

His round suns rose on their white beaches to stare

The world focused carefully on more important things

His blinking is the sound of small boys throwing crusts on the water

Teddy

for a child with leukaemia

Teddy was not well.

Teddy had been feeling sick.

Teddy had to go to hospital.

Teddy was told that he had too much blood.

Teddy did not miss his friends.

Teddy knew the thermometer was not sharp.

Teddy was not scared of needles.

Teddy said the medicine would make him better.

Teddy closed his eyes at night.

Teddy ate his vegetables.

Teddy's small girl lay in the corner of his bed.

She was not so sure.

Her eyes were made from round buttons.

The fluff on the top of her head was worn
as though it had been chewed.

Lost property

for a child with Diamond-Blackfan syndrome *

She was not left on the kitchen sink,
beside an open window,
cooling like a pie.

She was not left in a warm pocket,
pushed around by dull coins
into frayed holes.

She was not hung like ripe fruit
on a bent tree, dripping
over the back fence.

She did not talk carelessly to strangers.

She was wrapped in cotton wool,
kept in a locked safe,
held inside a careful room.

No-one saw her slip away.

God told me he spent the day
going through his books.

I did not see him when I looked.

* Diamond-Blackfan syndrome is a rare congenital blood disorder

The sparrow

*for a child with Noonan's syndrome**

Five times child

We picked you up off the ground

Out of the long grass

Out of the smell of damp leaves

Placed you in a matchbox
full of tissue paper

Fed you milk with an eye-dropper

Took you with us to school

Showed you to our mothers

Bought you a new set of clothes

Found you a nice job in a good office

Gave you the keys to the car

Chose a sensible woman to fall in love
with those brown eyes

Until we realized you were a bird

And must have been trying to fly.

* Noonan's syndrome is a congenital disorder associated
with heart disease, short stature and learning difficulties.

A mini mental status examination

1. She told me that it was summer and that we were in the south of France. Last night we had heard a man sing beautifully on the street and had sipped wine while we listened. Her father was important and young men had always sought her. I was no exception. She complained of the heat.

2. She remembered three things:

   One   The sound of crickets frying in the sun.
   Two   The correct way for casting on a row of stitches.
   Three That in her father's house were many mansions.

3. She told me that my pen was a dagger and that my watch was a fading rose in my hand.

4. She said that the world was already backwards and why make it worse.

5. She wrote: *Old Meg she was a gypsy*
   And lived upon the moors
   Her bed it was the brown heath turf
   And her house was out of doors.

6. She drew a butterfly on a piece of paper for me.
   She coloured the body in blue where the wings overlapped.

7. She closed one eye at a time slowly while she looked at me with a smile.

8. She took the paper in her right hand, screwed it up and threw it at me.

   No if's, and's or but's.

   Later I told her what day it was and the name of the place where we had talked.

   I said her name like a cold flannel wiping away the food from someone's mouth.

   There are times when I wonder why I did.

On the death of my grandmother

Joyce Lilias Colquhoun, 1915 – 2002

On the beach where I live, last Sunday
three children built a man out of sand.

He lay on his back with his arms by his sides,
his feet slightly spread as though he was asleep.

His eyes were made of two round shells.
His lips were the stick from an ice-block.
The tide eyed him like seagulls stalking bread.

He was both alive and dead at the same time.

The first wave touched his arm then
ran to see what he would do next.

The second pulled a finger
but again he did not stir.

The third wave ran between his legs as though
he was an old man pissing himself.

The fourth circled him, taking a layer
of sand equally from his right and
from his left so that he remained the same
shape as before but somehow smaller.

The fifth wave covered him and in between
its small currents turning he seemed to move.

The sixth wave took his lips.
They floated out to sea.
His eyes sank down to the back of his head.

The seventh wave made him look younger.

After the eighth wave he was the idea of a man.

The ninth wave wiped him off the beach like a cloth
on a table where children have been eating cake.

The tenth wave would never have known
that he had been there in the first place.

But I still say that he was:

In everything that I remember of him,

In one ice-block stick and two ordinary shells,

In this story which has just been told, and

In ten thousand small pieces of sand sprinkled
widely through a great and restless ocean.

'Amputation of a leg.' Johann Wechtlin, 1517.
Mary Evans Picture Library.

A woman with club feet

She walked awkwardly,
creased in half at the waist
                to keep balance,

her feet were bent like claws.

I thought it was not fair.

Then I saw the sun strike on her wings,

Her coat of brown feathers ripple in the breeze,

That proud head turn smoothly to the sea,

The speed with which she flew.

I saw the launch of her into swift air,

The strong and steady beat of her shoulders,

My reflection in her green eyes as she passed,

Her toes tucked quiet inside the wind.

Listening to the songs she sang
I had not heard before,

I thought it was not fair.

It was not fair at all.

Mothers, love your sons

Mothers, love your sons.
Love your big, dumb sons,
Your idiot sons,
Your swaggering sons,
Your awkward sons,
Your irresponsible sons and their indestructible limbs.

Love their red and bleeding knees.
Love their clear, uncluttered eyes.
Love their stumbling, foal-like hands.
Love their necks just asking to be wrung.

Love their shoes lost in the neighbour's yard.
Love their badly ironed clothes.
Love their terrible haircuts.
Love their empty tanks of petrol.

Love their awkwardness at airports leaving
for a world they were expecting to change.

Love their awkwardness at airports returning
from a world they were expecting to change.

Love the hair on their chins like
a small lawn of badly cut grass.

Love their broken-hearted girlfriends
calling in the middle of the night.

Love your northern sons,
Your southern sons,
Your eastern sons,
Your western sons.

Love your granite sons,
Your iron sons,
Your crystal sons,
Your paper sons.

Love your rising sons,
Your blazing sons,
Your noonday sons,
Your setting sons.

Mothers, love your sons.
Love your big, dumb sons,
Your idiot sons,
Your swaggering sons,
Your awkward sons,
Your irresponsible sons and their indestructible limbs.

Because they die so fast,

So awkwardly, lankily, idiotically, swaggeringly fast,
With everybody staring at them,
On a Friday night, with a wicked grin,
In the moment of their greatest triumph,

When they will always be the last to know,

The last, that is, except for you.

A short poem dictated one day by an intubated patient

I t i s j u s t t h a t m y f e e
t a r e c o l d a n d t h a t o
f m y c l a s s a t s c h o o l
i r e m e m b e r t h i r t y t
w o n a m e s a n d t h a t i f
e e l t h e s u n s h i n e w h
e n y o u t o u c h m e a n d
t h a t u n s p e a k a b l e c
o l o u r s o f f i s h s w i m
i n t h e s e a b y m y b e d

The crumbling patient

I glued her nose back on
with chewing gum.
Later — her hair fell out.

I taped the hair back to her head.
Her tongue stuck like a dagger
between my toes.

I wedged her tongue inside her mouth.
Her lips clung to the side of my hand.

Her arm clattered to the floor.
I secured it to her shoulder
with a drawing pin.

Her fingers came off in my hand.
I used them to hold the lips
back on her mouth.

Her eye bounced on the ground
and rolled underneath the bed.
I washed it in cold water
and stuck it back in place.

Her jaw dropped but held with
two small screws in each corner

which made her grin.

I made a spike out of her neck
and stuck her head back on.

A row of clips held up her skin.

I fastened her legs with an old hinge.

Her feet glued carefully
together like a broken vase.
Each crack was a vein.

I said goodbye.

And hoped she would not slam
the door on her way out.

'A woman representing knowledge examines a sick child.'
Lithograph by G. Tyr after A.J.V. Orsel. Wellcome
Library, London.

When the bell breaks

for a child with meningitis

That day I found you,
we both were lost.

Our floor was a hard cradle.

I waited beside your bed in the dark.

I listened for sounds of breathing.

I prodded you with a long stick.

I looked inside my book of plans
and traced a finger along a diagram.

I watched advertisements for glue.

I learnt the configuration of knots.

I made a tower out of used minutes.
Every one was a burnt match.

I discussed you with all the king's
horses and all the king's men.

They could not put you together again.

I hid you under the mat.

And asked you not to do this to me.

An examination of
her body after death

for Rongo Subritzky, 1913–1999

You are not her shoulders!
There has been a mistake!
The long, thick candles of Catholics
hold clammy in my hands.
Where are the rubbery veins?
These are made from brittle wax.

You are not her face!
What is going on?
Who has corrected the drawings of
children with expensive artists?
What has been done with their mistakes?

You are not her eyes!
Someone has slipped up!
These are broken headlights on a car.
Lock all the doors. Who has escaped
with the shining of the sun?

You are not her mouth!
Would someone please explain?
The sound of birds has gone away.
So bold! These two fat worms
now hungry for the dirt.

You are not her belly!
This is unacceptable!
I can hardly bear that plate of drying
sandwiches. There should have been
fresh fish heads boiling in a pot.
No wonder we are hungry.

You are not her thighs!
How could this have happened?
I remember clearly the kick of flounder
escaping through the net. These have
hung from loops of flax for too many days
on the back fence.

And you are not her feet!
I refuse to understand!
These toes are the upturned roots
of trees fallen over on the ground.
Hers would have cracked the earth in half.
At least would leave a larger hole to fill.

To a woman who fainted recently at a poetry reading

A blood pressure of ninety millimetres of mercury is normally required to adequately perfuse the central nervous system. If the head is lowered, however, the pressure needed to maintain consciousness is considerably lower. Of course if one has severed a major artery or torn it lengthwise like a weak seam in the lining of a jacket then poetry should not be blamed and, in fact, may become entirely appropriate.

It is wise to consider hypoglycaemia as a contributing factor. I have heard that a barley sugar placed per rectum in obtunded patients with a precipitously low serum glucose may at times mean the difference between them dying and never eating barley sugar again.

Simple dehydration, overheating or a sudden shock can also be associated with fainting. For this last reason poetry should not be left lying around especially if it is graphic in nature, with swear words in it like 'bugger' or 'bastard' or 'shit'. Lines such as 'She used to love me but now I am a crumb in the biscuit tin of life' can induce vomiting. 'She used to love me / My heart is the sound of oysters opening at low tide' can also be counted on to take the breath away.

Micturition syncope is a syndrome in which men who increase their intra-abdominal pressure at the moment of urination can impair their venous return, cardiac output and subsequently faint, however this cause will usually be obvious from the history and immediate setting. Individuals suffering in this manner can sometimes be confused with those who have drunk too much then pissed themselves before collapsing.

Despite a strong link between alcohol and poetry this scenario seems unlikely to be the case in your situation and so it only remains for me to write you the following prescription — four black wheels swallowed whole like pills; one siren, the blade of a sharp knife; three sheets, as crisp as biting apples, two flashing lights striking matches in the wind — and in this small ambulance send you, like flowers, straight to hospital.

'A woman passes out in the street.' Engraving by Bertall circa 1860. Mary Evans Picture Library.

Lines composed one day
underneath an anaesthetic machine

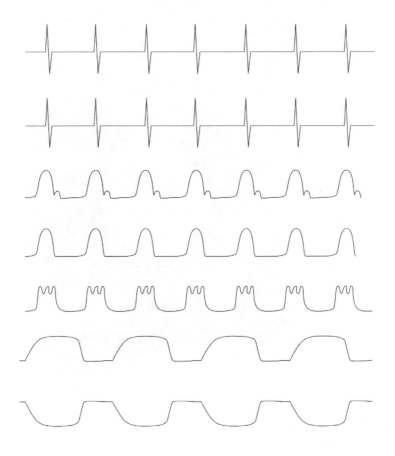

z z z z zꝲꝲꝲꝲz z z z zꝲꝲꝲꝲz z z z zꝲꝲꝲꝲz z z z zꝲꝲꝲꝲ

The earthquake

for a child with epilepsy

She was a small country
built on a fault line.

Her belly was a round field,

A farmer stepped out the
position of fenceposts.

Her feet were a coast,

They splashed wildly
when she played.

Her eyes were an ocean,
as blue as an unsailed sea.

Her face was a small town.

People drank coffee
on hot afternoons
in her streets

And did not notice
the slight roll of the spoons
on their saucers.

Parkinson's disease

for my father

I am poured out like water, and all my bones are out of joint:
my heart is like wax ... My strength is dried up like a potsherd:
and my tongue cleaveth to my jaws ... ~ **Psalm 22**

1. Whose disease is it anyway?

In the beginning
it was Mr Parkinson's,
A party trick at socials,
A bit of a laugh,
A shiver in a rock that
was strong and broad
and carried the sky
on its shoulders.

Later on, watching you
get up off the floor in pieces,
wedging your feet
underneath to balance,
I thought that maybe
this belonged to you.

At two o'clock in the morning
pushing your weight to the
shore of the bed —
where gravity laps,

> or at six o'clock at night
> watching you fall asleep
> in one conversation
> and wake up in the next,

>> or at any other o'clock after that
>> watching the drawn thread
>> pulled slowly at night
>> through my mother's smile again,

>>> I thought that maybe
>>> they should name it after us.

2. Multiple choice questions

(a) It could have been a virus
    he is still trying to shake.

(b) It could have been a rusted key
    in a lock that will not turn.

(c) It could have been a path over-
    grown in his mind with weeds.

(d) It could have been God stumb-
    ling over his extension lead.

(a) It could have been from thinking
    that he would always be strong.

(b) It could have been from laughing
    at his grandmother's bad knees.

(c) It could have been that someone
    cut his hair while he was sleeping.

(d) It could have been he liked to
    pour his concrete in bare feet.

(a) It could have been from curses
    placed by people that he hurt.

(b) It could have been a screw loose
    or a spanner in his works.

(c) It could have been his gutters
    filled with rubbish or with leaves.

(d) It could have been he might have
    fought with something he could see.

3. Shaking hands with Mr Parkinson

Shaking hands
with Mr Parkinson
is the longest meeting,

        hands beating
        60 per minute,
        or 3000 per hour,
        or 80,000 per day,

630 million altogether
give or take a few.

        They are slicing the
        world into small enough
        bundles to swallow.

They catch in the light
through the window.

        They fall on the ground
        between rain.

They blow through the
leaves of an old tree
making her dance.

        They catch in the shake
        of a wet dog.

I listen closely
to your hands in the wind
to see if they will sing.

4. Out on a limb

Did I ever tell you this man
used to make grape juice?

Once a year when
the grapes were sour.

He would boil them in a grey pot.

He would pour them through
cheesecloth which bled like
its heart had been opened.

He would squeeze the last drop
from a knot in the cloth.

He would splash the stove with juice.

His wife would help.

His children would watch all night.

He would scrape off the bits
which rose to the top.

He would bottle the rest.

They would wait on the shelves
like a calendar, removing the year.

When this happened the light in the
shed stayed on into the dark and

was safe. It has been a long time
since he drank the last bottle.

He still has the grey pot.

He still has the knot from which
he squeezes the last drops.

A man stopped me once and said
that when he had been young
they had called him 'Ox'.

"How is the Ox?" he said.
Have I ever told you that?

5. Slow motion

The man on television
scores in slow motion
as though he is running
through a pool
of chest deep water.

The details of his face
move into place
so obviously
they seem the changing
of scenery on a stage
between acts.

His arms pass through the air
the way that ants conduct crumbs
across the pattern on your tablecloth.

His legs are small children growing.

His hair is kelp against a coast.

Sweat trickles erratically
along his skin like footsteps
climbing backwards
down a ladder. Each drop
splashes carefully in time
with his heartbeat.

Ten,
Nine,
Eight,
Seven,
Six,
Five,
Four,
Three,
Two,
One,
Zero.

This is how my father pisses.

6. Transplantation

If I could take the beating of a wing out of the sky
or catch the thunder of rain off black tarseal,

if I could steal the glide of clouds
against the tallest building,
or the fury of a storm out at sea

I would tie them to this page — flapping.

I would mix them
with the anger of lightning
and of fading roses
and of longing.

I would melt them
with the flaming of leaves
on a blown tree,

with pieces of moon
dripped on the sea at night,

with the striking match of my pen.

I would boil them on the page
and screw it tight

to squeeze their moving bit by bit
inside your flesh.

I would sew you up quickly before they could get away.

I would stitch the wind under your skin
and leave you between the pot plants,

on the sill,

beside an open window.

7. The not getting better

When the tide goes out you will
see bit by bit the bottom of her life,

Crabs and shells and old tyres which
hold her up, her bare bones drying,

Holes which gulp quickly
their last drops of water.

There will be a less crisp line between the blue
and the white and the sun in the sky.

Fewer people will lay on the sand.

There will be a field of grey to walk on.

There will be a line of seaweed
to remind you of when the tide was full,
a line in the sand to say:

Here is as much as this man took for granted.

Between it and the water will be the other
landscape of his life, a place to find old bottles
and tins and pieces of wood covered by snails
and oysters and mud,

Bubbles where things live underneath,

All that the water hides.

Some will sit silently and wait
for the sea to return.

Some may walk in the mud with bare feet
and look under rocks for treasure.

DISEASES I HAVE KNOWN

Who can protect himself from harm and disaster
if he does not know his enemy?

~ *The nature of disease*, Paracelsus.

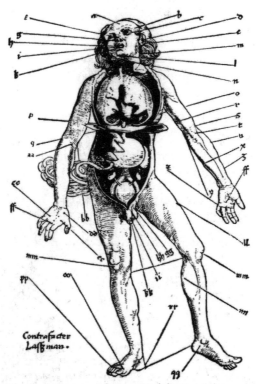

Bloodletting points. Johannes Wechtlin Treatise
on Surgery, 1540. Courtesy New York Academy of
Medicine Library.

Arthritis

Arthritis walks funny like a cowboy

through saloon doors
that curse behind his back
— *Goddammit all t'hell !*

Every joint chaws tabacca.

The floorboards creak.

His feet thud like walking sticks.

The bar leans out against him.

I pour his whiskey neat and say
How you been, Mr Arthritis?

He pokes his hat with the sharp end of his pistol
and says that he's seen better times.

For a while we watch long-legged girls
kick their thighs high into the air.

At night I watch him rest his head on a saddle.
His boots point up towards the moon.

Clouds tiptoe considerately across the sky.

His campfire glows dull red
for a long time in the dark.

Viruses

Viruses are my sister's children
who have come to stay at my place
for the weekend.

They try to get into the cupboards.

They draw with thick crayons
on the back of my throat.

They run up and down the inside of my head
with small hands covered in marmite and jam
which takes forever to get off the walls.

They bang pots and pans on the floor.

They wipe their feet on the centre of my tongue.

They cry loudly in the middle of the night.

Sometimes they swing
          on that dangly thing which hangs
                    from the back of my mouth

          until I cough.

I eat broken biscuits all week.

No wonder my nose runs.

The heart attack

The heart is not attacked
by red Indians clinging underneath
the bellies of their ponies.

The heart is not attacked by
kamikaze flying their exploding planes
onto its burning decks.

The heart is not infiltrated by secret agents
crawling through the air conditioning
into its secret chambers.

The heart is not broken
by the slippery hands of love.

The heart is not squeezed like
ripe lemons into a clean glass.

The heart is not beaten by
the arrangement of its soft belly
around a hard fist like a glove.

The heart is not stabbed by bayonets
or chainsaws or carefully sharpened kitchen knives
slipping their cold steel cleanly between its ribs.

The heart stops simply like a blocked toilet

While someone unsuspecting is opening the
newspaper or reading poetry or staring quietly at
the pictures in the calendar on the back of the door.

Sunday seems a good day for fishing.

A pair of trousers fall against the floor.

Leukaemia

You are a fish.
Slick bellied.
Round eyed.
Shell coloured.
Red gilled.
Almost beautiful.

You are a fish.
Lying still in the shallow curve of the spine.
Leaping high in the angry surf of the heart.
Waiting deep in the calm harbour of the belly.

You are a fish.
Thick bellied.
Dead eyed.
Hell coloured.
Dark gilled.
Almost beautiful.

You are a fish.
What bait has been
wasted on you.

Asthma

with thanks to Denis Glover

Not lions roaring impatient orders
at frightened waiters.

Not morepork chiming on the quarter-hour
from old abandoned clock towers.

Not snakes whispering gossip
concerning the minister's infidelities.

Not wolves calling after lovers
who have finally left them.

Not sheep nagging continuously at
frustrated parents for extra pocket money.

Not ducks disappointed that their men
will not get decent jobs.

Not dogs swearing loudly at cars who
continue to pull out in front of them.

Not cows snoring soundly
in front of their television sets.

This small boy has a flock of birds
let loose inside his chest.

*And quardle-oodle-ardle-wardle-doodle
the magpies said.*

Schizophrenia

Schizophrenia turns
off the television,

gets up from the couch,
puts on his coat,
opens the door,
walks down the road,

and buys a postcard
of New Zealand.

(it could be a calendar)
(it could be a T-shirt)
(it could be a photo in a book)

It is a picture of a mountain
and the lake below it.

He does not know what to look at.

The mountain in the sky, or the mountain in the lake. The mountain in the postcard,

or the mountain in his mind.

His hands reach out to touch
the water, or the ice, or
the cardboard, or his eyes.

When he turns around

the road walks him
back home again.

His door lets him in.
His coat takes him off.
His couch sits him down.

His television
switches itself on.

and watches him.

Heartsounds

sinus rhythm

THE heart
ROCKS like
AN empt
TEE chair
SOME one
HAS just
GOT up
TO leave.

second degree heart block

The heart dances
deliberately.
A hand rests gently
on its hip.

sinus arrhythmia

The heart batshereyelids at a boy.

atrial fibrillation

The heart
bangs
like a door
in the wind at
the
back of
the house.

ventricular tachycardia

The heart ticks like a clock on a bomb the hero has seconds to stop.

atrial flutter

Th eh ea rt is al ar ge ro om fu ll of pe op le cl ap pi ng.
Th es ou nd of ra in on at in ro of.

supraventricular tachycardia

Theheartisthevoiceofatrackannouncercallingacloseraceint
hefourthirtyatellerslieandthethunderofhoovesisexhilarating

third degree heart block

The heart is a smallchild practis ing the piano.

ventricular fibrillation

The heart
walks
        drunk
  from the back
door
         of a public bar
              and
fumbles
    with its fly.

asystole

The heart makes the whine of a kettle that has begun to boil.
Somewhere else the tea is getting cold.

The rash

The rash places an advertisement in the personal column of his local newspaper.

CULTURED, COLOURFUL, INFECTIOUS, BOLD, WITH AN ITCH ONLY YOU CAN SCRATCH. Into art, fashion, photography, architecture, design and graffiti. Give me a chance to grow on you, get underneath your skin, make an impression on you, inflame you.

A tattoo full of dull green fire licks down his forearm into the paper and burns the fingers of anyone who just happens to be turning the page at the time.

SPELLS

Desperate cases need the most desperate remedies

~ from *Aphorisms*, Hippocrates.

'A Medical Dispatch' by Thomas Rowlandson.
Wellcome Library, London.

A spell to be used when addressing the birth of a child

Let your first breath be
the volume of small lemons.

Let your second breath snap
like a sail in strong wind.

Let your third breath howl like a wolf
on the edge of a great mountain.

Let your fourth breath
hoot like an owl.

Let your fifth breath open slowly
like the eye of a wild animal.

Let your sixth breath
rise like the sun.

Let your seventh breath follow
the tide on its way out.

Let your eighth breath
guide it back in.

A spell to be used in the mending of broken bones

Blood turn black and blood turn blue
Fire turn cold and ice burn true
Devils stir and angels groan
Flesh meet flesh and bone meet bone.

Muscle bustle, muscle grow
Flow like rivers out of snow
Fill like arteries do with blood
Flow like rivers do in flood.

Tendon turn and tendon twist
Silver like a silver fish
Be old women knitting twine
Five-six-seven-eight-and-nine.

Bone be woman, bone be man
Bone reach out your bony hands
Tangle gently lips on lips
Twist forever hips round hips.

Blood turn black and blood turn blue
Fire turn cold and ice burn true
Devils stir and angels groan
Flesh meet flesh and bone meet bone.

Increasingly sophisticated methods of divination used in the practice of medicine

By observing a rooster pecking grain.
By the various behaviours of birds.
By balancing a stone on a red-hot axe.
By the shape of molten wax dripped into water.

By the pattern of shadows cast onto plastic.
By the colour of paper dipped in urine.
By the growing of fresh mould in round dishes.
By the magnification of blood.

By the alignment of electricity around the outside of the heart.
By the rise in a column of mercury.
By timing exactly the formation of clots.
By the examination of excrement.

By the placement of sharp needles underneath the skin.
By tapping the knee with a hammer.
By the bouncing of sound against a full bladder.
By the interpretations of pus.

By the attractions of the body to strong magnets.
By the characteristics of sweat.
By listening carefully to the directions of blood.
By waiting to see what happens next.

A haka to be used when reversing the effects of a general anaesthetic

Feet!
Be the fingers of piano players.

Hips!
Be the mouths of two lovers.

Belly!
Be the faces of children.

Arms!
Be the legs of strong runners.

Neck!
Be the forearms of axemen.

Lips!
Be the bellies of round snakes.

Eyes!
Be the tongues of small kittens.

Heart!
Be the feet of a dancer.

A curse to place on viruses, bacteria, parasites, fungi and all other infectious disease

Typhus get diphtheria,
Diphtheria, the pox,
Varicella get malaria,
Malaria get spots.

Spots get salmonella,
Salmonella, gonorrhoea,
Gonorrhoea get legionella,
Legionella, diarrhoea.

Shigella get yersinia,
Yersinia, the mumps,
Mumps contract listeria,
Listeria get lumps.

Lumps contract pneumonia,
Pneumonia get thrush,
Thrush contract giardia,
Giardia get flushed.

Measles get E.coli,
E.coli, leprosy,
Trichomonas, rotavirus,
Pseudomonas or TB.

TB get influenza,
Influenza, treponemes.
And if nothing else
will stop you

Then I wish you
human beings.

An attempt to prevent
the death of an old woman

Old woman, don't go, don't
go outside into dark weather
Out into the night's wet throat
There is cooking on your stove
Old woman, don't go.

Don't go old woman, don't go
Down beneath that deep sea
Down onto its soft bed
There are still fish to be caught
Old woman, don't go.

Don't go old woman, don't go
Bent into that slippery wind
Listening for its clean voice
There are songs still left to sing
Old woman, don't go.

Don't go old woman, don't go
Walking beside that steep cliff
Watching where the sea flowers
There are daisies on your lawn
Old woman, don't go.

Don't go old woman, don't go
Lifting in those strange arms
Caught against that dark chest
There are people left to hold
Don't go, old woman, don't go.

A spell to be cast prior to dying

Die, go on, time's up, die.

Die naked as the day you were born. Die stitched up beautifully in silk. Die for better. Die for worse. Die richer. Die poorer. Die in sickness and die in health. Die running with your arms outstretched cheering. Die being carried or hauled or dragged kicking and screaming to the front end of the queue.

Die without anybody noticing it. Shrivel away until there is nothing at all. Leave your keys on the kitchen sink and slip surreptitiously out the back door. Then again die gigantically, with sirens and whistles and the explosion of fireworks, small birds stopping on their way home to take notice.

Die peacefully, the way fat angels are painted by distinguished artists on the ceilings of churches, as if they were lying back inside the sky instead of hanging half blissfully out of it. Die enormously pissed off as though you were a player complaining about the referee after a game lost in the last minute or a child whose best toy has just been broken.

Die in agony, screaming blue bloody murder, throwing the pills you have been given to make you feel better at their terrified doctors, hurling abuse at nuns who are only trying to do their job. On the other hand die without even knowing you have died like a marriage that has continued for too long, read about it with surprise in the magazine you keep in order to live as you do through the sins of someone else.

Die lingering like the arrangements for a wedding you can't wait to be over or die suddenly and without warning while you are watching the result of the penalty shoot out after extra time in a cup final that is played only once every four years.

Die while you are asleep dreaming about chocolate or sex or world domination or die while you are most awake, at that point when you realize the final number in the lottery draw matches the one you have always been waiting for.

Die looking backwards as though you were somehow desperate to get off the tracks when the train finally hit or die looking forward thinking about the next line in a song while you are singing the one before it.

Die as if you deserved it the way a bushranger waits stoically, his eyes clear as hope before the gallows, or die as though it was an incredible injustice, stomping to your room after the money missing from your mother's purse was found in your innocent drawer.

Die as if death was a complete stranger knocking on your door like a Jehovah's Witness peddling his inconvenient literature. Die as if death was the skin of a lover, tickled and tempted and teased, smooth as water drunk on a hot day.

That's all I want to say, die, go on, get the hell out of here, find your own way home.

Die, die as if your whole life depended on it.

A spell to be used in the event of a cardiac arrest

Call to the ember
in the fire
growing dull.

Call to the plain girl
not dancing.

Call to the fish
on the end
of its line.

Call to the soldier
not marching.

Call to the bird
singing weak
in the tree.

Call to the broomstick
not sweeping.

Call to the child
still awake
in the dark.

Call for the child
who is sleeping.

A PORTRAIT OF THE DOCTOR
AS A YOUNG MAN

Life is short, science is long: opportunity is elusive, experiment is dangerous, judgement is difficult. It is not enough for the physician to do what is necessary, but the patient and the attendants must do their part as well, and circumstances must be favourable.

~ *Aphorisms*, Hippocrates

'Protective Clothing of Doctors and Others Who Visit Plague-Houses.' c.1720, from Dr François Chicoyneau. Wellcome Library, London.

A medical education

for Peter Rothwell

In obstetrics I learnt that a woman opens swiftly like an elevator door. The body wriggles free like people leaving an office on a wet afternoon.

In surgery I learnt that the body is an animal. The heart paces slowly like a tiger in its cage.

In medicine I learnt that the body is the inside of a watch. We hunch carefully over small tables with blunt instruments.

In geriatrics I saw that the neck becomes the shape of an apple core.

In A&E I learnt that the body is a fish. Some gasped for air as though they had been caught.

In paediatrics I learnt that the body is a bird. I leave small pieces of bread in smooth trails.

In intensive care I discovered that the body is a number. The sick sweat like schoolboys studying maths before a test.

In radiology I saw that the body is a map.

In orthopaedics I found the body can be broken. Bones make angles under skin as though they were part of a collapsed tent.

By patients I was shown the body is an instrument. Some have played the finest music.

In anaesthetics I saw people hang on narrow stalks like ripe apples.

But in the delivery suite I learnt to swear.

A brief format to be used
when consulting with patients

The patient will talk.

The doctor will talk.

The doctor will listen while
the patient is talking.

The patient will listen while
the doctor is talking.

The patient will think that the doctor
knows what the doctor is talking about.

The doctor will think that the patient
knows what the patient is talking about.

The patient will think that the doctor
knows what the patient is talking about.

The doctor will think that the patient
knows what the doctor is talking about.

The doctor will be sure.
The patient will be sure.

The patient will be sure.
The doctor will be sure.

Shouldn't hurt a bit, should it?

Today I do not want to be a doctor

Today I do not want to be a doctor.

No one is getting any better.

Those who were well are sick again
And those who were sick are sicker.

The dying think that they will live.
And the healthy think they are dying.

Someone has taken too many pills.
Someone has not taken enough.

A woman is losing her husband.
A husband is losing his wife.

The lame want to walk.
The blind want to drive.
The deaf are making too much noise.
The depressed are not making enough.

The asthmatics are smoking.
The alcoholics are drinking.
The diabetics are eating chocolate.

The mad are beginning to make sense.

Everybody's cholesterol is high.

Disease will not listen to me

Even when I shake my fist.

Today I want to be a doctor

Today I am happy to be a doctor

Everyone seems to be getting better.

Those who were sick are not so sick
And those who were well are thriving.

The healthy are grateful to be alive.
And the dying are at peace with their dying.

No one has taken too many pills.
No one has taken too few.

A woman is returning to her husband.
A husband is returning to his wife.

The lame accept chairs.
The blind ask for dogs.
The deaf are listening to music.
The depressed are tapping their feet.

The asthmatics have stopped smoking.
The alcoholics have stopped drinking.
The diabetics are eating apples.

The mad are beginning to make sense.

Nobody's cholesterol is high.

Disease has gone weak at the knees.

I expect him to make an appointment.

'The Reward of Cruelty' by Hogarth, 1751, showing the dissection
of a hanged criminal. Mary Evans Picture Library.

Taking confessions

Forgive me doctor for I have sinned.
It has been three months since my last condition.

I have stepped on the point of a nail.
I have swallowed the bone of a chicken.
I have beaten my thumb with a hammer.

The father, the son and a bottle of spirit.

Forgive me doctor for I have sinned.
It has been three months since my last infection.

I have walked outside in cold weather.
I have allowed my carpets to remain damp.
I have stood in the pathways of those who do
not cover their mouths when they cough.

The pharynx, the lung and the alveolus.

Forgive me doctor for I have sinned.
It has been three months since my last erection.

I have dwelt on the centres of slick magazines.
I have watched cattle sex vigorously in fresh fields.
I have seen chimneys on tall buildings billow smoke.

A harlot, some fun and the bloody Mrs.

Forgive me doctor for I have sinned.
It has been three months since my last depression.

I have argued about dogs with my neighbours.
I have forgotten the names of my children.
I have broken my heart on a lover.

The pharmacist, Jung and a chocolate biscuit.

The morning after
a night spent taking blood

The girl in the shop wraps
groceries in newspaper

with fingers as familiar
at making change,
or applying make-up,

or flicking long
brown hair through an
elastic band to hold it.

Her skin might have been
smooth like the desert.

The top of her dress might
have leant like a small fence
against her breast.

She might have looked with
warm brown eyes at me.

All I saw was the way one
vein leapt like a taut fish

from the soft slack sea in
the crook of her arm

and those long thin cords
flung onto the back of her

hand like dreadlocks
sleeping on a pillow.

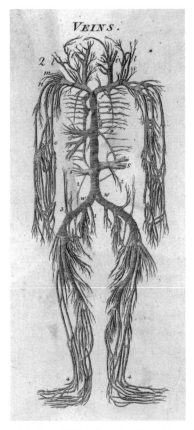

Unnamed Artist. mid 18th Century. Mary Evans Picture
Library.

A painting on the wall of the radiology department at Waikato Hospital

It is one hundred and seventeen
years since Mary Cassatt
painted a picture of two
children playing on the beach.

They will have got up,
walked down to the sea,
washed the sand off their feet,
only for it to collect again
like frost on an ice-block
left too long in the freezer.

Later they will fall in love, or not,
get married, or not,
have children of their own, or possibly none,
look at art, grow old and die
still feeling the same age
as that day on the beach,
sand running through their fingers,

And the fingers of the man standing
in the corridor of a hospital,
smelling the salt rubbed sharp into the air,

Wondering if his poem lasts
one hundred and seventeen years
what various days he might have fallen
into and then out of again,

Whether people will still feel the
same as he, the same as her, the
same as they, confronted by a beach,
a bucket and spade, the sea turning,
the gulls rolling, feet being bared,

And if over the intervening years when
so much must inevitably have changed
this should always remain the same.

PLAYING GOD

I swear by Apollo the healer, by Aesculapius, by Health
and all the powers of healing, and call to witness all the
gods and goddesses that I may keep this Oath and Promise
to the best of my ability and judgement.

~ from the Hippocratic Oath

'Christ curing a suppliant of blindness.' 14th century Ethiopian
miniature, courtesy World Health Organisation, Geneva.

1. Creation

On the first day God won the toss and put me in to bat. I discovered blood was pumped around the body by the heart. I found powerful drugs to keep it flowing. I pioneered cardiac transplantation. God was ridiculed by the press and the selectors were put under pressure.

On the second day God took performance enhancing drugs which I was able to detect from metabolites in his urine. He would not supply a second sample. The public were suspicious.

On the third day I proved the cellular structure of the human body. God collapsed the scrum and broke my neck which I was able to repair with six months traction and the grafting of new nerves from baby pigs. People said it was a miracle.

On the fourth day I discovered penicillin. God's bishop was removed. God adopted a two knight's defence and turned his pawns into horses which began to storm down the back straight. God told Mrs God that he had kicked my arse. I pointed to the scoreboard.

On the fifth day God struck dead the umpire. I brought him back to life with one milligram of adrenaline. God asked me who the hell I thought I was. He spent ten minutes in the sin-bin and was fined half his match fee.

On the sixth day I discovered DNA. God went down on his knees. I sequenced the human genome and cloned myself. The crowd went wild. God said in the newspaper that he did not want to play any more.

On the seventh day bacteria were made resistant to antibiotics. New viruses were discovered in Africa. The drinking age was lowered. In a regular column the *British Medical Journal* reported a large increase in deaths attributed to earthquakes, pestilence, lightning, famine and flood.

2. Communion

There will be tea in a mug.

I will make it on the table in front of him. We will talk about high blood pressure and how the fish are biting. He will discuss the changes to dairy farming during the period 1945–1975 and how they have impacted heavily on the rural sector. He will forget the sugar then tell me it could eventually kill me.

There will be tea in a cup.

The cup will have roses on it. The sugar will be well stirred. A small measure of tea will spill onto the saucer which matches the cup it usually rests beneath in the glass-panelled cabinet beside the piano. We will talk about cats and strokes and getting old.

He will talk about Aucklanders and his 'prostrate.'

Both annoy him. I will be offered a beer which will be refused apologetically before I have answered. Tea will eventually come in a pot with a silver spout. He will have to excuse himself as it is poured.

She will provide bacon, eggs, sausages and chips with scones and raspberry jam.

I will be given a glass of Fanta because I am a boy. We will talk about high cholesterol, ischaemic heart disease and recent blood tests. She will tell me it is marvellous what my tests can tell.

I will tell her three things remain:

Aspirin,
Surgery,
And a cup of tea,

but the greatest of these
is a cup of tea.

3. Performing miracles

The heart is stitched
laboriously into place by sharp
needles and fine thread.

The lungs are cleaned
by stiff brooms and bossy cleaners
throwing open all its windows.

The kidneys are emptied
without glamour down the drainpipes
of a thousand kitchen sinks.

The brain is kept working
by the ladies on the
local switchboard.

All miracles here
are usually performed
by various members of
the domestic staff.

4. The carpenter

The skin is acceptable as far as skin is concerned. It is better than paper but inferior to tape. It is too easily torn. There is too much variation in colour. It is ill-fitting, inflammable, too tight, too loose and unpredictable when touched. It would be better if it was replaced by a disposable, clear plastic wrap that washes out in soapy water. Through this may be seen more clearly the machinery of the heart.

The intestines will do for now. They are better than a garden hose left kinking in the sun but easily improved upon with a few simple household items. You will need the inner tubes of four tyres, one brightly coloured beach ball, the large end of any brass instrument such as a trumpet, tuba or trombone, one bicycle horn, and a cork taken cleanly from the sharp end of a bottle of wine.

The eyes can always be used in the manner for which they were intended. They are better than dark glasses worn by young men on still nights to appear casual but with minimal adjustment their usefulness can be more fully extended. You will need one roll of thirty-five millimetre film, the headlights from a late model car, two windscreen wiper blades, one packet of jelly crystals and a box of brightly coloured crayons.

The bladder should not be made to feel unappreciated. It is superior to the rusted tanks found at the back of infrequently used farmhouses but with a little imagination it can be easily made more efficient. Collect one teapot, the washers from four taps, five lengths of copper spouting, one spanner, a handful of nuts, six drinking straws, one garden sprinkler, and three cans of CRC.

The heart is to be tolerated if that is all that is available. It is better than a school child practising loudly their accordion but inferior to a more reliable physiology which can be simply achieved from the valves of four Captain Cooker pigs. You will also need forty metres of plain rubber tubing, the pendulum of a grandfather clock, the belly of one recently purchased hot water bottle and a set of AAA batteries. Any residual cavity in the chest may be packed by one or two pairs of clean socks. As yet there is no solution available for the longing which surrounds the human heart.

5. The judge (or, Some choices to be made when separating Siamese twins joined at the heart)

The left eyes are blue.
Blue is the colour of the sky.
Robert Redford has blue eyes.
Blue eyes leap out of the head and arrest me.
There is a song playing on the radio
about a person who has blue eyes.

The right eyes are brown.
Brown is the colour of chocolate.
Brown eyes sink inside the head
like small caves I want to explore.
There is a song playing on the radio
about a person who has brown eyes.

The left mouth is open.
An open window lets in sun.
The left mouth is discussing the cure
to a rare illness or explaining a recipe for
cake or singing a song so beautiful
that a whole generation will cry.

The right mouth is closed.
A closed window keeps out rain.
The right mouth is keeping a secret on
which you depend or administering
lipstick or solving the algebra of
travel through time.

The left forearms are muscular,
thick ropes holding large ships to a pier.
The left forearms are rescuing small
children from burning buildings or keeping
away burglars or hitting the ball as far
as possible out of Candlestick park.

                    The right forearms are graceful,
                    the pathway of tears along make-up
                    or the neck of a horse eating grass.
            The right forearms are playing the piano
                    or shaping soft clay or sewing back
                    life into somebody's heart.

The left thighs are pohutukawa.
Pohutukawa grow crooked by the sea.
Their bark is the face of an old man.
One is the shape of an old woman
weeding her garden. Even she does
not know where to place this axe.

                    The right thighs are kauri.
            One particular kauri is known as The Lord
            of the Forest. His mother was made out of
                    soil and his father was wide like the sky.
            One day he tore them apart with his roots.
                    Sometimes gods can be devils too.

LOS MÉDICOS VISITAN A UN APESTADO.
DE LA CHIRURGIA, DE BRUNSCHWIG, 1500

'A physician and two assistants attending a patient ill
with plague.' Lithographic reproduction of a woodcut.
Wellcome Library, London.

6. When I am in doubt

When I am in doubt
I talk to surgeons.
I know they will know what to do.

They seem so sure.

Once I talked to a surgeon.
He said that when he is in doubt
He talks to priests.
Priests will know what to do.

Priests seem so sure.

Once I talked to a priest.
He said that when he is in doubt
He talks to God.
God will know what to do.

God seems so sure.

Once I talked to God.
He said that when he is in doubt
He thinks of me.
He says I will know what to do.

I seem so sure.

7. Myths

Please do not be disappointed
but when I go home
I do not live in a batcave.
There are no figure-hugging capes
hanging in my wardrobe.
There is no utility belt
for last minute escapes.
There is no butler, no batmobile,
no Robin, no orphaned life,
no Holy this, no Holy that,
no holiness at all.

It is not my intention
to distress you
but when I go home
I do not live inside a bottle.
I do not sleep with a gun
underneath my pillow.
I do not change my clothes
in a telephone box or switch off
a nuclear device taped to
the thighs of a beautiful woman.
I do not collect any messages
which threaten to self
destruct in five seconds.
I have been both
shaken and stirred.

I am sorry to have to break
this news but when I go home
I have to look in books.
I try hard to remember
the pathways of arteries.
I forget the names of bones.
I get mixed up between
my right and my left.
I wish I had used a different drug.
I consider what would have happened if
I had put the needle in the other arm.
I wonder if you are alive or dead.

Try not to be alarmed
but when I go home
I do not turn the water into wine.
I do not eat with tax collectors.
I usually forget to say grace.
My father was a carpenter but
he has never owned a donkey.
My mother was not a virgin
when I was born but she would
not want me to dwell on that.
If this is a cause of concern
to you please do not
hang me on a cross.
Contrary to popular opinion
I cannot raise the dead.

8. Playing God

If you play God, play God at tennis.

A strict code of conduct is expected.
Clear lines must be drawn in the sand.
The ball will be either in or out.
At times there is talk of love.

If you play God, play God at chess.

All decisions must be black or white.
There are ways for him to be kept in check.
Bishops are available for consultation.
There is the possibility of mating.

If you play God, play God at darts.

He will dislike their resemblance to nails.
An acceptable target must be provided.
There is a fine line he will not be permitted
to cross. Cursing should never be allowed.

If you play God, play God at monopoly.

Everyone will be expected to take turns.
He must sit at a table like everyone else.
You might refuse him a room at your inn.
He is certain to be feeling overconfident.

9. A note of warning to patients when all else fails

Sometimes the needle is too blunt.
The stethoscope is too quiet.
The scalpel will not cut.
The scissors chew like old men's gums.

Sometimes the book has not been written.
The pill cannot be swallowed.
The crutches are too short.
The x-rays hide like dirty windows.

Sometimes the thermometer will not rise.
The plaster will not stick.
The stitches cannot hold.
The heart conducts a normal ECG.

Then I have to ask you what to do

Which is what you might
have wanted all along.

Notes

Notes

Also from Hammersmith Press

Suburban Shaman
tales from medicine's frontline
By Cecil Helman
194 pp
ISBN: 978-1-905140-08-4

'Medicine is not just about science. It's also all about
stories, and about the mingling of narratives among
doctors, and between them and their patients.'

So writes Cecil Helman after 27 years as a family
practitioner in and around London interlaced with training
and research as a medical anthropologist, comparing a
wide variety of medical systems and other forms of healing.

This unique combination of frontline health worker and
detached academic informs the many stories that make up
this fascinating book. It also informs the author's insights
into what human suffering can teach us about ourselves
and our own attitudes to health and illness, whether we are
deliverers or recipients of health care.

With insight and compassion, Dr Helman's stories take the reader on a journey from apartheid South Africa, where he did his medical training, to the London of the early 1970s, where for a short time he foreswore medicine to become an anthropologist and poet; from ship's doctor on a Mediterranean cruise to family practitioner in London; from observing curative trance dances in the favelas of Brazil to interviewing sangomas in South Africa.

While trained in the Western tradition and with many years of practice in that system, Dr Helman's anthropological insight leads him to view illness in a wider personal, social and cultural context, considering elements beyond the purely physical. In pleading for this holistic approach he celebrates family medicine which 'in its quiet and unassuming way, and every day of the week, is still at the very frontline of human suffering'.

Also from Hammersmith Press

The Medical Miscellany
By Manoj Ramachandran & Max Ronson
174 pp
ISBN: 1-905140-05-3

This fascinating collection of medically-related items will inform, tantalize and infuriate you by turns. How can you tell if a murder victim was left- or right-handed? How many euphemisms can you think of for unmentionable parts of the body? What has chicken pox got to do with chickens? And does a famous doctor or medical scientist share your birthday?

We challenge you not to find something unexpected on every page, nor to smile or groan at almost every entry. How much do you know? How much will you be able to remember?

About Hammersmith Press Ltd

An independent publisher providing books on matters relating to medicine, health and nutrition for the specialist and non-specialist reader

Hammersmith Press is an independent publishing house producing books for the general public and health professionals that deal with the interface between medicine and complementary approaches to health care, including nutrition. Many of our books offer an integrated approach (e.g. Chronic Fatigue Syndrome – a natural way to treat M.E.) while others take a critical look at Western medicine (e.g. Suburban Shaman – tales from medicine's frontline) and still others take a critical look at complementary therapies (Traditional Herbal Medicines – a guide to their safer use).

Founded in 2004, we see a need for books that address readers as interested, intelligent custodians of their own health who want to have thorough explanations of the advice they are given rather than taking guidance on trust.